Faith Quest

Bible Tales for Little Explorers

The Birth of Jesus

This book belongs to

Summary

In this beautifully illustrated retelling of the first Christmas, children will journey to Bethlehem to witness the miraculous birth of Jesus, the Savior of the world. Follow Mary and Joseph as they travel to Bethlehem, where baby Jesus is born in a humble stable. Meet the shepherds in the fields, who are visited by a host of angels announcing the joyous news. Then, travel from afar with the wise men, guided by a shining star, as they bring gifts to honor the newborn King. This heartwarming story celebrates love, peace, and the miracle of Christmas, sharing the true meaning of the holiday with children everywhere.

The Angel Gabriel Visits Mary

Once upon a time, in a small village called Nazareth, there lived a young woman named Mary. Mary was kind-hearted, humble, and loved by everyone in the village. She spent her days helping her family, tending to the animals, and praying to God. Mary believed that God had a special plan for everyone, though she never imagined He would have an extra special one for her!

One day, as Mary sat by the window weaving a basket, something incredible happened. A soft glow began to fill the room, and Mary noticed that the light seemed to shine brighter and brighter, but it didn't hurt her eyes at all. It was a warm and comforting light, like the sun on a cool day.

Suddenly, right before her eyes, a tall and majestic angel appeared, dressed in robes as white as snow. His wings were wide and shimmering like the morning dew, and his face was radiant with peace and kindness. Mary gasped in amazement, for she knew that she was standing in the presence of an angel.

"Do not be afraid, Mary," the angel said in a gentle voice. "I am Gabriel, and I come with a message from God."

Mary's heart was pounding, but she could feel the love and peace flowing from the angel's words. She bowed her head, humbled that God would send an angel to speak to her.

"The Lord is with you," Gabriel continued, "and you are greatly blessed among women."

Mary looked up at the angel, her eyes wide with wonder. She couldn't understand why God would choose her. "What does this mean?" she asked softly.

Gabriel smiled and spoke again. "Do not be afraid, Mary. God has chosen you for something very special. You will have a baby, a son, and you are to name him Jesus. He will be great and will be called the Son of the Most High. His kingdom will never end, and He will save the people from their sins."

Mary's heart raced. She felt joy and confusion all at once. How could this be? She wasn't even married yet! She was engaged to a kind man named Joseph, but they had not yet started their family.

"How will this happen?" Mary asked Gabriel, her voice trembling.

The angel's face remained calm and full of light. "The Holy Spirit will come upon you, and the power of the Most High will overshadow you. The child born to you will be holy, the Son of God."

Mary's mind was filled with questions, but her faith in God was greater than her fear. She had always trusted God's plans, even when they seemed impossible. Taking a deep breath, she looked up at Gabriel and said, "I am the Lord's servant. May it be as you have said."

Gabriel smiled brightly, his wings fluttering ever so slightly. "You have found favor with God, Mary. He is with you, and you will do great things."

And just like that, the angel vanished, leaving Mary alone in her small room, but not afraid. Instead, she felt a deep peace and joy. She knew her life would never be the same. She was carrying a great secret, one that would change the world forever.

Mary spent the rest of her day in quiet reflection, thanking God for trusting her with such a wonderful gift. She thought about the baby, her precious Jesus, who would grow to be a king not just of their land, but of the hearts of all people. Mary knew that this was the beginning of a beautiful and miraculous journey.

And so, from that day forward, Mary carried the promise of God, knowing that the child she would soon welcome into the world would be the Savior of all.

The Journey to Elizabeth's Home

Mary needed to talk to someone, someone she loved and trusted. She thought of her cousin Elizabeth, who lived in the hill country, far away from Nazareth. Mary knew that Elizabeth would understand what she was feeling. So, without delay, Mary packed a small bag, and with a joyful heart, she set out on her journey. The road to Elizabeth's house was long and winding, leading through hills and valleys. But Mary didn't mind. She was excited to see her cousin and share the wonderful news.

As Mary walked, she hummed softly to herself, her heart overflowing with joy. She thought about the baby growing inside her and the promise that God had made. She knew that her visit with Elizabeth would bring comfort and peace.

The sun shone brightly, and the air smelled sweet with wildflowers as Mary made her way through the countryside. She imagined the look on Elizabeth's face when she told her everything the angel had said. Mary smiled to herself, feeling a sense of peace and wonder.

After several days of traveling, Mary finally reached the little village where Elizabeth lived. She hurried to the house, her heart beating with excitement as she knocked on the door.

Elizabeth came to the door, her face lighting up with surprise and happiness when she saw Mary standing there.

"Mary! What a wonderful surprise!" Elizabeth exclaimed. Her smile was warm and welcoming, and she quickly invited Mary inside.

But before Mary could even say a word, something amazing happened. As soon as Mary stepped into the house, Elizabeth felt her baby leap with joy inside her! It was as if baby John knew that Mary was carrying someone very special—Jesus, the Son of God.

Elizabeth gasped in amazement and placed her hands on her belly. She looked at Mary with shining eyes and said, "Blessed are you among women, and blessed is the child you will bear! But why am I so favored, that the mother of my Lord should come to me? As soon as I heard your voice, the baby in my womb leaped for joy."

Mary was overwhelmed with happiness. Elizabeth knew! God had revealed the truth to her before Mary even had a chance to tell her. Mary's heart was filled with gratitude as she realized that Elizabeth understood just how special this moment was.

In that moment, Mary felt so full of joy and thankfulness that she couldn't help but sing. With Elizabeth by her side, Mary lifted her voice in praise to God. Her song was full of love and trust in God's plan:

"My soul glorifies the Lord,
And my spirit rejoices in God my Savior,
For He has been mindful
Of the humble state of His servant.
From now on all generations will call me blessed,
For the Mighty One has done great things for me—
Holy is His name."

Mary's song echoed through the house, filling the air with praise and gratitude. She sang of God's goodness, His mercy, and His promises. She knew that God had a plan for her, for Elizabeth, and for the whole world through the baby she was carrying.

Elizabeth listened with tears in her eyes, feeling the same joy and awe that Mary did. She, too, knew that God's plan was unfolding in ways greater than they could ever imagine.

Mary stayed with Elizabeth for several months, and their time together was filled with love, joy, and lots of talking about the wonderful things God was doing in their lives. Every day, they marveled at how God had blessed them both with these miraculous babies—John, who would prepare the way for Jesus, and Jesus, who would save the world.

The two cousins spent many hours sitting together, feeling their babies move inside them and talking about what the future would hold. Elizabeth was so happy to have Mary with her during this special time, and Mary was grateful to be with someone who understood what she was going through.

Together, they laughed, prayed, and dreamed about the incredible future their children would have. Elizabeth's home became a place of peace and joy, filled with the love of God.

When it was time for Mary to return to Nazareth, she hugged Elizabeth tightly. "Thank you for everything," Mary said with a smile. "I will never forget this time we spent together." Elizabeth smiled back and said, "God has great plans for you, Mary. I know you will be a wonderful mother to Jesus."

With a heart full of joy and faith, Mary began her journey home, knowing that God was guiding her every step of the way.

And so, as Mary walked back to Nazareth, she carried not only the baby Jesus in her womb but also the love and encouragement she had received from her dear cousin Elizabeth. She knew that no matter what lay ahead, God's plan was unfolding perfectly, and she was part of something far greater than she could ever imagine.

Mary Tells Joseph and the Angel Gabriel Visits Him

Mary was filled with joy and wonder after the angel Gabriel's visit. She carried the incredible news in her heart: she would soon give birth to a baby boy, the Son of God. But even though she trusted God's plan, there was one person she needed to tell—her beloved fiancé, Joseph.

Joseph was a kind and hardworking carpenter. He was a good man, honest and thoughtful, and he loved Mary deeply. They had promised to marry, and he was busy preparing their future home, making sure everything would be perfect for the day they became husband and wife.

One evening, as the sun was setting over Nazareth, Mary decided it was time to tell Joseph what had happened. Her heart pounded as she walked to his workshop, where the rhythmic sounds of his hammer echoed through the air.

"Joseph," Mary said softly, stepping into the doorway. Joseph looked up, smiling as he wiped his hands on his apron. But when he saw the seriousness in her eyes, his smile faded slightly. He could tell something was on her mind.

"Is everything alright, Mary?" he asked, concerned.

Mary took a deep breath, her hands trembling a little as she sat down. "I have something important to tell you," she began, her voice steady but quiet. "An angel came to me—a messenger from God."

Joseph listened carefully, but he was confused. "An angel?"

"Yes," Mary continued. "The angel told me that I am going to have a baby, but this is no ordinary child, Joseph. The angel said the Holy Spirit will overshadow me, and this child will be the Son of God. His name will be Jesus, and He will save our people."

Joseph's eyes widened in shock. He didn't know what to say. Mary was telling him something incredible, something beyond understanding. How could this be? They weren't yet married, and Mary was saying she was going to have a baby.

His mind swirled with questions and doubt. He loved Mary, but this news was overwhelming. He wasn't sure what to think or feel. Without a word, he stood up and left the workshop, his heart heavy with uncertainty. He cared for Mary deeply, but this news changed everything.

That night, Joseph lay in bed, unable to sleep. His thoughts kept racing. He loved Mary, but what she told him seemed impossible. He was a good man and didn't want to embarrass her, but he also couldn't ignore what was happening. Maybe it was best to quietly end the engagement and let her go.

As Joseph wrestled with his decision, something miraculous happened. Just as Mary had been visited by an angel, so too was Joseph.

In the stillness of the night, a bright, comforting light filled Joseph's room. Startled, he sat up, his eyes wide as he realized he wasn't alone. Standing before him was the angel Gabriel, radiant with light and peace. Joseph felt a deep sense of awe and calm wash over him.

"Joseph, son of David," the angel said in a gentle voice, "do not be afraid to take Mary as your wife. The child she is carrying is from the Holy Spirit. She will give birth to a son, and you are to name him Jesus, because He will save His people from their sins."

Joseph's heart slowed as the angel's words settled over him. It was all true—everything Mary had said. This child was no ordinary baby; He was the promised Messiah, the Savior. The angel continued, "This fulfills the prophecy: 'The virgin will conceive and give birth to a son, and they will call him Emmanuel, which means 'God with us.'"

With those words, the angel's light began to fade, and soon, Joseph was left alone in the quiet of the night. But now, his heart was at peace. The doubts that had once filled his mind were gone. He knew what he needed to do.

The next morning, Joseph rushed to see Mary. His heart was light, and his spirit filled with hope and joy. When he saw her, he took her hands in his and smiled, his eyes shining with love.

"Mary," he said softly, "the angel came to me, too. I understand now. God's plan is greater than anything we could have imagined. I will stand by you, and we will raise this child together. He will be called Jesus, just as the angel said."

Tears of relief filled Mary's eyes as she smiled up at Joseph. Her heart overflowed with gratitude and love, knowing that Joseph believed her, and that he would be by her side for the incredible journey ahead.

And so, Joseph and Mary prepared for the birth of Jesus, knowing they were part of something far greater than themselves—God's great plan to bring love, light, and salvation to the world.

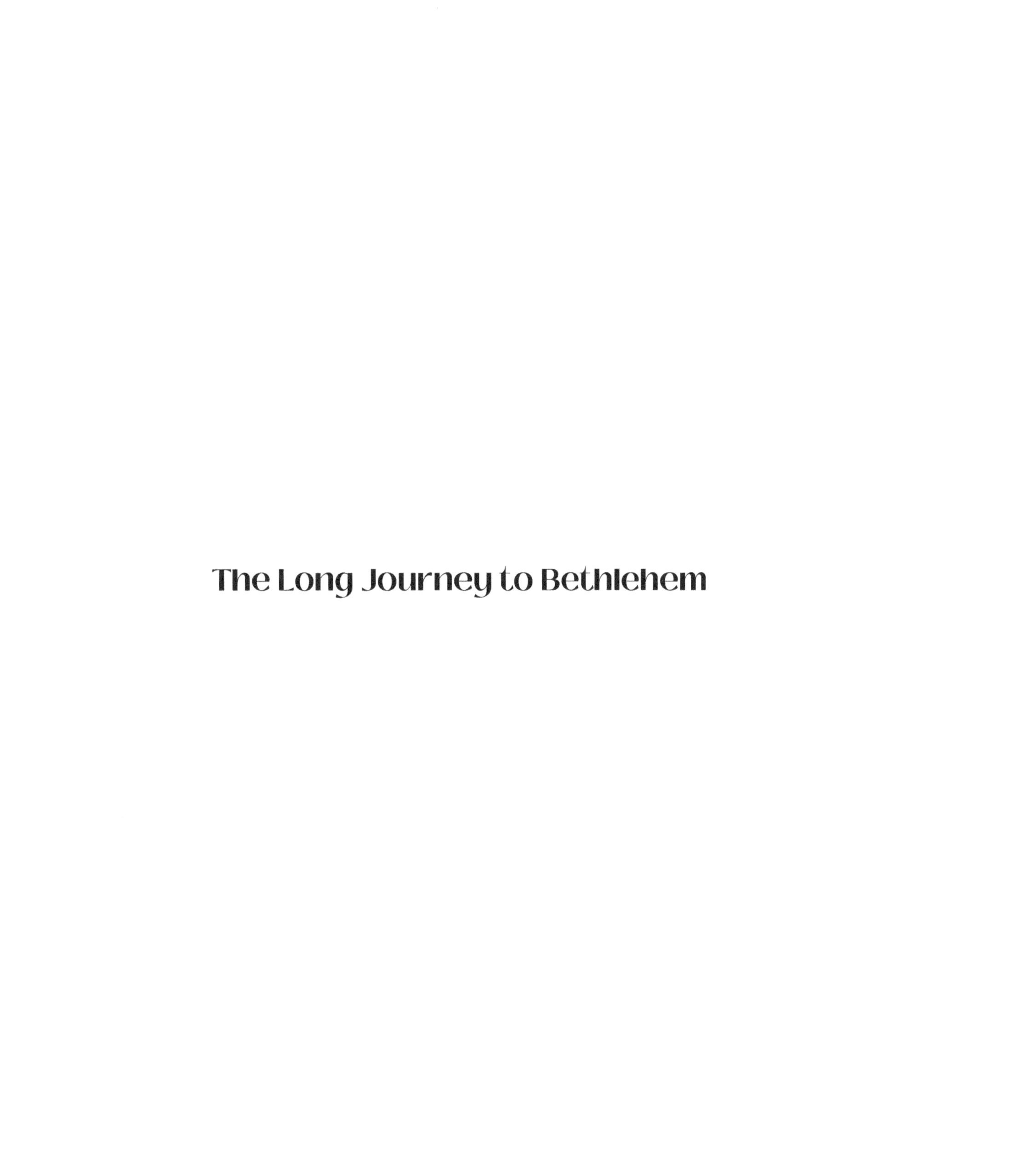

The Long Journey to Bethlehem

Mary and Joseph had been so excited as they made plans for the baby's arrival. Joseph, a kind and hardworking carpenter, had been building a little crib and making their home just right. Mary was preparing everything with love, knowing that the baby she was carrying was a gift from God.

But just when they thought they had everything ready, something unexpected happened.

One morning, a messenger came through the village with news from the Roman emperor, Caesar Augustus. He had ordered everyone in the land to return to their hometowns to be counted for a census. Since Joseph's family was from Bethlehem, a town far away from Nazareth, he and Mary had to pack up and make the long journey there.

Mary looked at her round belly. The baby would be arriving soon, and traveling such a long way wouldn't be easy. But Joseph reassured her, "God is with us, Mary. He will take care of us on this journey." And deep in her heart, Mary knew Joseph was right. They trusted that God would protect them and their soon-to-be-born child.

Early one morning, Joseph helped Mary onto a gentle donkey. The sun was just beginning to rise, and the sky glowed with soft pink and orange colors. Mary sat comfortably on the donkey's back while Joseph led the way. Their path would take them over hills, through valleys, and across dusty roads as they traveled to Bethlehem.

The journey was long and tiring. Mary's back ached, and the baby felt heavy inside her. The road was rocky, and every bump made Mary hold her belly, feeling the baby move. Sometimes, the winds blew strong, and other times the sun shone so brightly that it made them both feel hot and tired. But whenever Mary started to feel weary, Joseph would say with a kind smile, "We're almost there. God is with us."

At night, they would rest under the stars. Joseph would find a safe place where Mary could sit, and he would spread out a blanket for her to lie on. The stars above twinkled like diamonds, and sometimes, Mary would hum softly, thinking about the baby in her belly. She knew He would be very special, and she felt peace even in the middle of their long and difficult journey.

Joseph would often look up at the sky too, wondering about the amazing things that would happen when Jesus was born. He couldn't believe that he and Mary had been chosen to be part of such an important plan. He thought of the angel's words from his dream, "Do not be afraid to take Mary as your wife. The child she carries is from the Holy Spirit."

Those words gave him strength whenever he felt tired. God had a special plan for them, and he would take care of Mary and the baby no matter how far they had to travel.

After many days and nights of traveling, they finally saw the little town of Bethlehem in the distance. Joseph breathed a sigh of relief. They were almost there!

But as they got closer to the town, Joseph began to worry. So many people had come to Bethlehem because of the census that the streets were full, and the inns were crowded. Joseph knocked on door after door, trying to find a place for them to stay.

"Do you have a room for us?" Joseph asked the innkeepers. "My wife is expecting a baby soon, and we've traveled a long way."

But each time, the answer was the same. "I'm sorry, but there's no room left."

Mary was tired, and Joseph grew more and more concerned. He didn't want Mary to give birth out in the cold night air with no shelter for her or the baby. But he continued searching, knocking on every door, praying for help.

Finally, one kind innkeeper looked at Mary with compassion and said, "I don't have a room inside, but there is a stable in the back. It's not much, but it's warm, and there's plenty of hay for you to rest on."

Joseph thanked the innkeeper, grateful for anything at this point. He quickly led Mary to the stable, where the gentle animals—cows, donkeys, and sheep—watched quietly as they entered. The stable smelled of fresh hay, and the soft glow of lanterns made it feel cozy despite being a barn.

Joseph spread out fresh straw for Mary to lie down on, and together, they made a little bed of hay. It wasn't what they had imagined for the birth of their baby, but they knew God had led them there for a reason.

That very night, in the stillness of the stable, something miraculous happened. Mary felt the baby begin to move, and soon after, she gave birth to a beautiful, healthy baby boy. They wrapped Him in soft cloths and placed Him in the little manger—a feeding trough for the animals—because there was no crib.

The baby's eyes twinkled, and His face was peaceful and calm. As Mary looked down at Him, her heart swelled with love. She knew that this tiny baby was the Son of God, just as the angel had told her. Joseph, too, felt a deep sense of wonder and joy as he gazed at the newborn child. This was Jesus, the Savior who would bring light and hope to the whole world.

As they rested in the stable, the sound of the animals softly munching hay, the peaceful night outside, and the glowing warmth from their lantern made everything feel just right. Even though they weren't in a grand palace or a warm inn, Mary and Joseph knew they were exactly where God wanted them to be.

That night, as the stars shone brightly over Bethlehem, Mary and Joseph sat together in the stable, gazing at the baby Jesus with hearts full of love, peace, and hope for what was to come.

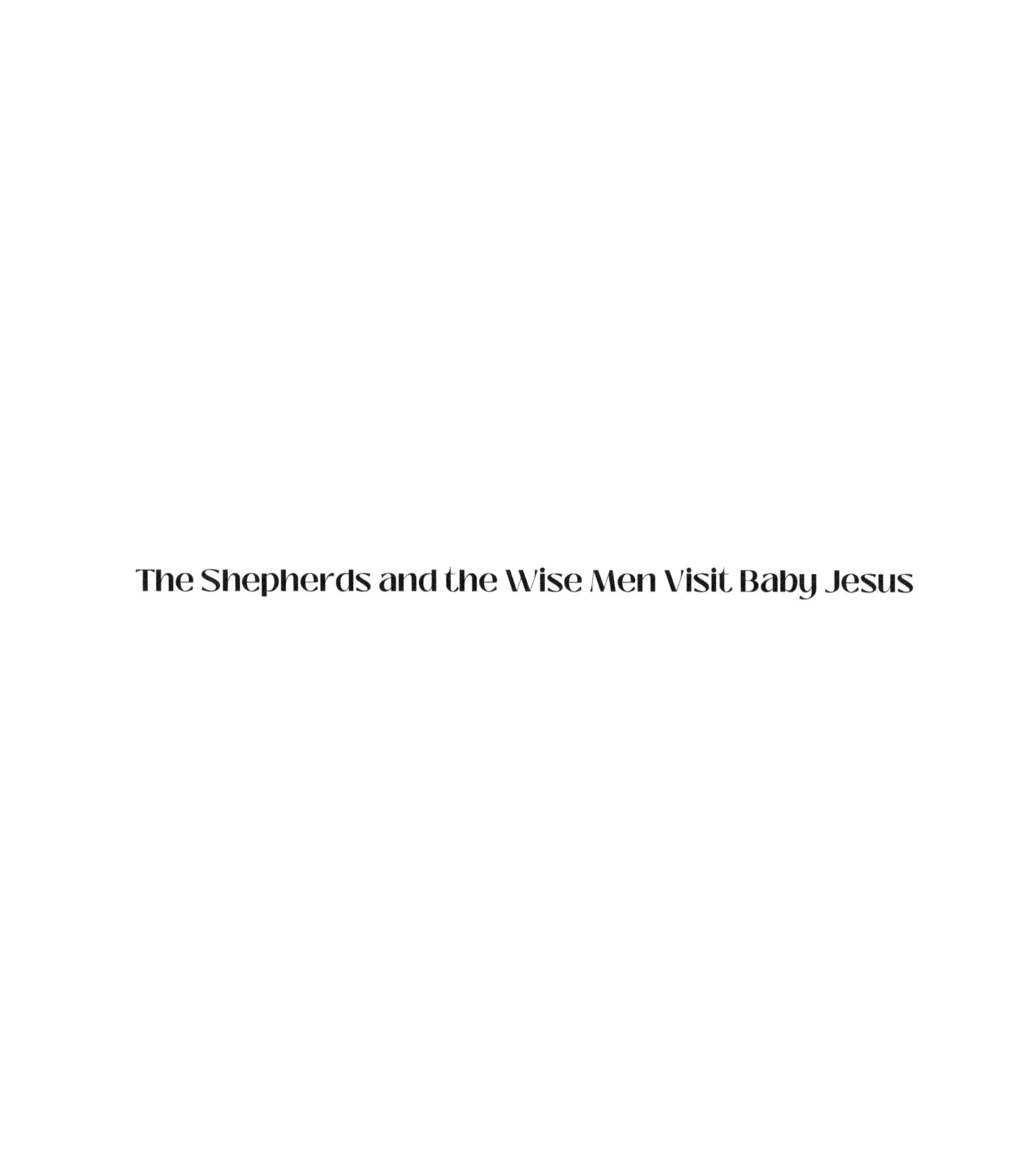

The Shepherds and the Wise Men Visit Baby Jesus

On the same night that Jesus was born, outside Bethlehem, there were shepherds sitting in the fields, watching over their sheep. The night was quiet, and the stars twinkled overhead. The shepherds were talking and tending to the fire when, all of a sudden, something incredible happened!

The sky lit up with a brilliant light, and an angel appeared! The shepherds were so surprised, they could hardly believe their eyes. They had never seen anything like it before! The angel had a bright, glowing face and a gentle smile. The shepherds were a little scared at first, but the angel spoke kindly to them.

"Do not be afraid," the angel said. "I bring you good news that will make everyone happy! Today, in Bethlehem, a Savior has been born. He is Christ the Lord. You will find Him wrapped in cloths and lying in a manger."

Just as the shepherds were beginning to understand, the sky filled with even more angels! There were hundreds of them, maybe thousands, singing together:

"Glory to God in the highest,
And peace on earth to those with whom God is pleased."

The shepherds stood amazed, watching and listening to the heavenly song. When the angels disappeared, the night sky returned to its usual calm, but the shepherds' hearts were racing with excitement.

"We have to go to Bethlehem!" one of the shepherds said. "We have to see this baby the angels told us about!"

So, leaving their sheep behind, the shepherds hurried to Bethlehem to find the special baby.

The shepherds followed the angel's words and soon found the stable where Mary, Joseph, and baby Jesus were resting. There, just as the angel had said, they saw the newborn baby wrapped in swaddling cloths and lying in a manger.

The shepherds knelt down in awe. They had never seen such a precious sight. This tiny baby was the Savior of the world, the one they had been waiting for! With big smiles on their faces and joy in their hearts, they quietly thanked God for letting them be a part of this special night.

After they spent some time with Mary, Joseph, and baby Jesus, the shepherds left to share the good news with everyone they could find. As they ran through the streets of Bethlehem, they told people, "We've seen the Savior! The angels told us He's here, and we saw Him with our own eyes!"

Everyone who heard their story was amazed, and the shepherds continued to praise and thank God for everything they had experienced that night.

Far away from Bethlehem, in a land to the east, there were wise men, or Magi, who spent their days studying the stars. One night, as they were looking up at the sky, they saw something they had never seen before: a bright, shining star, bigger and brighter than any other star.

The wise men were curious. They knew this star was special, a sign of something important.

"This star means that a great king has been born," one of them said. "We must follow it and find Him."

So, the wise men packed their bags and began a long journey to find the newborn king. They traveled for days and days, crossing deserts and mountains, always keeping the bright star in sight. Along the way, they thought about the gifts they would bring for the king. After all, this wasn't just any king—this was a king who would change the world.

The wise men decided to bring three very special gifts:

Gold: A gift for a king.
Frankincense: A sweet-smelling incense, used in worship.
Myrrh: A valuable oil often used for anointing.

After a long journey, the wise men finally arrived in Bethlehem. The star they had been following stopped right over the place where Mary, Joseph, and Jesus were staying. With excitement in their hearts, the wise men entered the house, and there they saw Jesus, no longer a newborn, but still a little baby, sitting on His mother's lap.

The wise men knelt down in worship, recognizing that this was not just any child—He was the King of Kings! They carefully placed their gifts before Him: the gold, the frankincense, and the myrrh. Mary and Joseph were amazed to see these important visitors from far away, and they thanked God for bringing them safely to meet Jesus.

The wise men were filled with joy as they looked at the baby. They knew their long journey had been worth it. They could sense the great importance of this moment, knowing that this little baby was destined to bring love and peace to the whole world.

After their visit with Jesus, the wise men were ready to return home. But that night, something remarkable happened. In a dream, God warned them not to go back the way they came, because the wicked King Herod was searching for Jesus and wanted to harm Him.

So, the wise men obeyed God's warning. Instead of returning to King Herod, they took a different route back to their home, keeping the location of the baby Jesus safe.

Mary and Joseph were amazed by all the visitors who came to see their little baby. First, the humble shepherds, who had heard the news from the angels, and then the wise men from far away, guided by a shining star. Each visit showed how special Jesus was and how God was watching over Him.

The shepherds and wise men returned to their homes, filled with joy and wonder. Everywhere they went, they told people about what they had seen: the baby Jesus, who had been born to bring light, hope, and love to the world.

And so, the good news of Jesus' birth spread far and wide, bringing joy to people everywhere. It was the beginning of a story that would change the world forever—a story of God's great love for all people, young and old, rich and poor.

A Detailed Chronology of Jesus's Birth

The story of the birth of Jesus is a beautiful and miraculous event that unfolds within the context of God's plan to bring salvation to the world through His Son, Jesus. From the moment the angel Gabriel visited Mary to the birth of Jesus in Bethlehem, each stage of her pregnancy is filled with wonder, faith, and divine purpose. Below is a detailed chronology of the key moments in Mary's pregnancy, based on biblical accounts from the Gospels of Matthew and Luke.

1. The Annunciation (Luke 1:26–38)

Event: The angel Gabriel visits Mary.
Time: About 9 months before Jesus' birth.

Mary was a young woman, likely a teenager, living in Nazareth when the angel Gabriel appeared to her. Gabriel told Mary that she had found favor with God and that she would conceive and give birth to a son, whom she would name Jesus. The angel explained that the baby would be the Son of the Most High and that His kingdom would never end.

Mary was puzzled and asked how this could happen since she was a virgin. Gabriel reassured her, saying that the Holy Spirit would come upon her and that the child would be conceived by God's power. Gabriel also told Mary that her cousin Elizabeth, who had been barren, was six months pregnant with a baby in her old age.

Filled with faith and humility, Mary responded, "I am the Lord's servant. May your word to me be fulfilled." And with that, the angel left her.

2. Mary Visits Elizabeth (Luke 1:39–56)

Event: Mary travels to visit her cousin Elizabeth.
Time: Likely early in Mary's pregnancy, within the first few weeks.

Shortly after the angel's visit, Mary set out to visit her cousin Elizabeth, who lived in the hill country of Judea. Elizabeth was about six months pregnant with John the Baptist when Mary arrived.

As soon as Mary greeted Elizabeth, Elizabeth felt her baby leap with joy in her womb. Filled with the Holy Spirit, Elizabeth recognized that Mary was carrying the Lord and exclaimed, "Blessed are you among women, and blessed is the child you will bear!"

In response, Mary sang a beautiful song of praise to God, often called the "Magnificat." She stayed with Elizabeth for about three months, likely helping her as Elizabeth neared the end of her pregnancy, and returned home just before Elizabeth gave birth to John the Baptist.

3. Joseph Learns of Mary's Pregnancy (Matthew 1:18–25)

Event: Joseph is visited by an angel in a dream.
Time: Shortly after Mary's return from Elizabeth's home, likely within the first few months of her pregnancy.

When Mary returned to Nazareth, it became clear that she was pregnant. Joseph, her betrothed, was a righteous man and didn't want to disgrace Mary publicly, so he quietly considered calling off their engagement.

But one night, while Joseph was asleep, an angel of the Lord appeared to him in a dream. The angel told Joseph that Mary's child had been conceived by the Holy Spirit and that the baby would be a Savior. The angel told Joseph to name the baby "Jesus," which means "The Lord saves."

When Joseph awoke, he did exactly as the angel commanded. He took Mary as his wife but did not consummate their marriage until after Jesus was born. Joseph trusted God's plan and accepted his role as the earthly father of Jesus.

4. Mary's Pregnancy Progresses in Nazareth

Event: Mary and Joseph prepare for Jesus' birth.
Time: Middle stages of pregnancy, months 4-8.

During the middle months of Mary's pregnancy, she and Joseph likely prepared for the arrival of their baby. Joseph, being a carpenter, may have been working on building furniture for their home and preparing a space for the newborn. Mary, like all expectant mothers, would have experienced the growth of her belly as the baby inside her grew.

Throughout this time, Mary and Joseph would have been surrounded by whispers from the community, as people knew that Mary's pregnancy began before their marriage. Despite this, both Mary and Joseph remained faithful to God's plan, trusting that His purpose was far greater than any gossip or misunderstanding.

5. The Census and Journey to Bethlehem (Luke 2:1-5)

Event: Mary and Joseph travel to Bethlehem for the census.
Time: Near the end of Mary's pregnancy, around 8-9 months.

Just as Mary was nearing the end of her pregnancy, the Roman emperor, Caesar Augustus, issued a decree that a census should be taken of the entire Roman world. This meant that everyone had to return to their ancestral towns to be counted.

Since Joseph's family was from Bethlehem, the city of David, he and Mary had to travel from Nazareth to Bethlehem, a journey of about 70-90 miles. This would have been a difficult trip for Mary, especially in the final stages of her pregnancy. She likely rode on a donkey while Joseph walked beside her, guiding the way.

Despite the long and tiring journey, Mary and Joseph trusted that God would take care of them. They knew that this census was part of God's greater plan, as it fulfilled the prophecy that the Messiah would be born in Bethlehem.

6. Arriving in Bethlehem and Jesus' Birth (Luke 2:6–7)

Event: Mary gives birth to Jesus in Bethlehem.
Time: The final days of pregnancy, just before or during the ninth month.

When Mary and Joseph arrived in Bethlehem, the town was crowded with people who had come for the census. Every inn was full, and there was no room for them anywhere. Finally, they found shelter in a stable, where animals were kept. It was in this humble and unexpected place that Mary went into labor.

In the quiet of the night, Mary gave birth to her baby boy—Jesus. She wrapped Him in swaddling cloths and laid Him in a manger, a feeding trough for the animals, because there was no crib. This was the long-awaited moment when God's promise was fulfilled. The Savior of the world had been born!

7. The Shepherds' Visit (Luke 2:8–20)

Event: Shepherds come to see the newborn Jesus.
Time: Shortly after Jesus' birth, possibly within hours or days.

While Mary and Joseph were marveling at the newborn Jesus, angels appeared to shepherds in the fields nearby. The angels announced the good news of Jesus' birth, saying, "Do not be afraid. I bring you good news that will cause great joy for all the people. Today in the town of David, a Savior has been born to you; He is the Messiah, the Lord."

The shepherds hurried to Bethlehem to see this miraculous baby. When they arrived at the stable and saw Mary, Joseph, and the baby Jesus lying in the manger, they were filled with awe. They worshiped Jesus and spread the word about what they had seen.

About the Author

Hello, I am C Brutus, I was born in Haiti in October 1992. Upon relocating to the United States, I pursued my education and embraced a diverse range of roles and accomplishments. Balancing the responsibilities of a devoted mother to two daughters and a supportive Navy wife, I handle my family duties with grace and resilience. In my professional life, I work with special education students, showcasing my dedication to inclusivity and education. Beyond the classroom, my love for learning and teaching led me to become a successful author. My collection includes various books like coloring books, activity books, and storybooks, all crafted to engage and inspire young minds. I am truly grateful for your support. A big thank you to my amazing customers for backing my small business endeavors.

Thank you!

C Brutus